The Great American Kid's Afghan is another in our series of afghans from the pages of past issues of *Knitter's Magazine* (issues 56–59). The squares are designed by North American knitters for their children and grandchildren.

This fun and portable project offers a wide variety of knitting and embellishment techniques that are clearly described and illustrated. Beginning and experienced knitters alike will find these afghan squares interesting to make—and great for honing your skills.

Even if you only know how to knit and purl we will guide you through the rest of the process. Learning is fun, especially when you knit in bright kid-friendly colors. Kids will have fun too, when they discover the special surprises awaiting them in this cuddly blanket.

Washable yarns in wonderful colors

CASCADE YARNS **Sierra**
80% Pima Cotton, 20% Wool
3.5oz (100g); 191yds (175m)
26, 19, 06, 52, 431, and 30

CHOOSE to make it yours!

Choose
the best
yarn

Choose
a **color**
palette

CASCADE YARNS **Sierra**
80% Pima Cotton, 20% Wool
3.5oz (100g); 191yds (175m)
eraser to pencil point
21, 429, 434, 22, 23, and 26

CASCADE YARNS **Pacific**
40% Superwash Merino Wool, 60% Acrylic
3.5oz (100g); 213yds (195m)
Spray can bottom to top
40 Teal, 35 Brown, 33 Green, 38 Purple, 43 Ruby
Red, and 22 Golden Yellow

1 2 3 **4** 5 6
Worsted weight yarn

220 Superwash
100% Superwash Wool;
3.5oz (100g); 220yds (200m)

*Colors of yarn and approximate yardage
to work the sample afghan.*
904 Deep Denim, 475 yds
877 Gold, 425 yds
1922 Ruby Red, 400 yds
854 Indigo, 300 yds
804 Purple, 250 yds
841 Avocado, 175 yds
12 balls total

10cm/4"

26
18
over stockinette stitch (knit
on RS, purl on WS), using size
5mm(US8) needles

**Sizes 6, 7, 8
(4mm, 4.5mm, 5mm)**
see instructions for details

2 **Size 9 (5.5mm)**
for edging

&
Tapestry needle

CASCADE YARNS **Sierra**
80% Pima Cotton, 20% Wool
3.5oz (100g); 191yds (175m)
15, 17, 29, 30, 405, and 423

Getting started

1 Don't think of all of these squares as equals. Some are fairly simple, others a bit more challenging.

2 You don't need to make an exact copy of our afghan. Arrange the squares any way you like. You may choose to repeat several of your favorite squares, or build your afghan with just one pattern.

3 Adjust the number of squares to suit your project; a few more squares make a child's bedspread. One square makes an ideal pillow. Back it with a plain square or a second square.

4 Due to the nature of the various patterns, all squares may not block to an exact 12" square. When sewn together, small differences in size will ease into shape.

5 Unless otherwise noted, the gauge is 18 stitches and 26 rows to 4" stockinette stitch (knit on RS, purl on WS), using size 5mm(US8) needles. If a square has a different gauge or uses a different needle size, it will be noted. As always, the needle sizes listed are merely a starting point; choose the needle size that gives you the correct stockinette stitch gauge and adjust the others accordingly.

6 Most squares begin and end with 3 ridges (6 rows) of garter stitch (knit every row) and have a 3-stitch garter border at each side edge.

Afghan finished measurements 36" x 48"

1	2	3
4	5	6
7	8	9
10	11	12

Square size 12" x 12"

Warm up on the easiest squares, and work your way up to the more challenging squares.

Finishing the afghan

Blocking the squares

Pin square to 12" and steam; never place the iron directly onto your knit piece. Or better yet, wash each square and pin out to dry. Then the squares will be clean and blocked.

Seaming the afghan

Sew squares together using grid shown above, fudging a bit if necessary. Use a strand of the most prominent color of the two squares you are join-ing. We found it most successful to seam from the right side. Place pieces side by side, with right sides facing you. Thread blunt needle with yarn to match piece.

Edging

Note *Edging is applied to afghan after all squares have been sewn together. On the sample afghan, the attached I-cord was worked with the WS of the afghan facing.*

Beginning at one edge of a middle square with Deep Denim and 2 double-pointed needles (dpn), work 3-stitch Attached I-cord around entire piece, taking care to pick up enough edge stitches so that the cord lies flat. Bind off I-cord and join to beginning I-cord as invisibly as possible.

Care

An easy way to wash a large piece like an afghan in a top-loading washer is to fill washer with warm water, add Eucalan (a non-rinse wool wash), then afghan. Let soak as directed. Do not agitate or rinse. Skip directly to spin cycle. Lay flat to dry. (Floor covered with towels works well).

Choose the size of afghan

Choose to omit/repeat one/several squares

Choose your own arrangement of squares

Seaming cast-on to bind-off

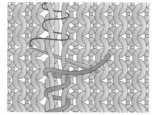

1 Pick up or catch a front leg of cast-on (right piece, above).

2 Cross to matching place on other piece and pick up or catch a front loop on bind-off (left piece, above).

3 Repeat steps 1 & 2 pulling thread taut as you go.

Seaming garter edges

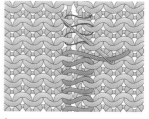

1 Pick up or catch a lower garter ridge from one piece (right piece, above).

2 Cross to matching place on other piece and pick up or catch an up-per garter ridge (left piece, above).

3 Repeat Steps 1 & 2, pulling thread taut as you go.

Attached I-cord

1 With dpn, cast on 3, then pick up and knit 1 stitch along edge of piece—4 stitches.

2 Slide stitches to opposite end of dpn and k2, then k2tog through the back loops, pick up and knit 1 from edge. Repeat Row 2 for I-corrd.

Nancy J. Thomas

JERSEY CITY, NEW JERSEY

You may know me as the former editor of Knitter's and not as a designer. But to celebrate the birth of my first grandson, I stepped out of my usual role to create a square in his honor. So Caprice, the star in our lives who we dearly love (thus, a big fuchsia heart), this one's for you!

Like many others, I learned to knit early in life and was taught by my mentor and grandmother. She was such a wonderful influence in my life. She loved all sorts of needlework and showed me how to enjoy the act of making something with my hands—whether it be embroidering a pillowcase, knitting socks, making a loaf of bread, or growing flowers.

Note *See page 28 for unfamiliar abbreviations and techniques.*

Square

With MC, cast on 54. Knit 6 rows (3 ridges garter stitch), end with a WS row. Keeping first and last 3 stitches in garter stitch, work center 48 stitches as follows: work 6 rows in Stockinette stitch (knit on RS, purl on WS), then begin to work 47 rows of chart, work 6 rows in stockinette stitch. Knit 6 rows. Bind off.

EASY +

featuring
simple intarsia

MC Deep Denim
A Gold
B Ruby Red

5mm/US 8
or size to obtain gauge

Stitch key
☐ Knit on RS, purl on WS
⊟ Purl on RS, knit on WS

Color key
▨ Deep Denim
☐ Gold
■ Ruby Red

Chart note: Begin working intarsia on Row 6 of chart. Use a strand of blue for right background area, a length of yellow for the right leg of star, a second length of blue for the center background, a second yellow for the left leg of star and a third length for the left background area.

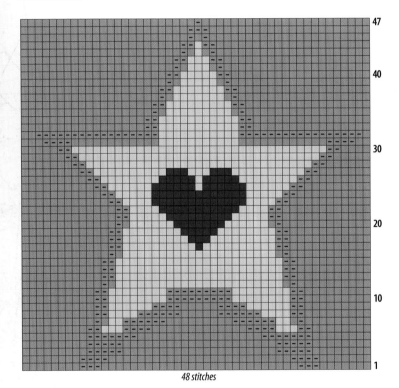

48 stitches

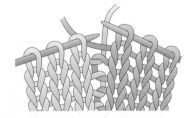
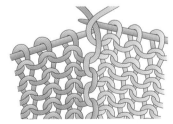

Intarsia basics

This is color-block or picture knitting. Each block of color is made with its own length of yarn. When changing from one color to the next, it is necessary to twist the yarns to prevent holes. Pick up the new color from under the old color, as shown, and continue working, following the chart.

Julia Grunau

TORONTO, ONTARIO, CANADA

During the early '80s I lived in the medieval Italian town of Siena in Tuscany. I loved it so much that I named my daughter after the city: Siena Elizabeth.

In her honor, this square contains motifs and patterns from the city's main cathedral, the Duomo, a riot of monochromatic texture and 2-color graphics This square's cabled columns echo those on 100-year-old mosaics in the cathedral's interior. The seed-stitch panels recall the decorative carved stone.

This piece is an excellent introduction to both duplicate stitch and 2-stitch cables, called 1/1 Right Twist and 1/1 Left Twist. It is worth learning to do as much cabling as possible without cable needles, and this square should give you enough practice to become confident.

Note *See page 28 for unfamiliar abbreviations and techniques.*

Square

With MC, cast on 55. Knit 6 rows (3 ridges garter stitch), end with a WS row. *Next row* (RS) Knit, increase 8 stitches evenly across—63 stitches. *Begin pattern: Rows 1 and 3* (WS) K3, **[p6, k1, p1, k1, p5, k1, p1, k1]** 3 times, p6, k3. *2* K3, ***[1/1 RT]** 3 times, k1, p1, k7, p1, k1, **[1/1 LT]** 3 times *****, k1, p1, k7, p1, k1, work from ***** to ***** once more, k3. *4* K3, *****k1, **[1/1 RT]** twice, k2, p1, k7, p1, k2, **[1/1 LT]** twice, k1 *****, k1, p1, k7, p1, k1, work from ***** to ***** once more, k3. Work these 4 rows 17 more times, then work Rows 1 and 2 once. *Next row* (WS) Knit, decrease 8 stitches evenly across—55 stitches. Knit 6 rows. Bind off.

Chart A

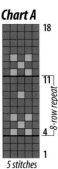

18

11

8-row repeat

4

1

5 stitches

Chart B

8

6-row repeat

3

1

5 stitches

☐ *Work duplicate stitch in CC*

1/1 LEFT TWIST With right needle behind left needle, knit 2nd stitch on left needle through back loop, then knit into front of first stitch; slip both stitches off needle.

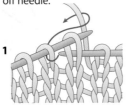

1

2

3

1/1 RIGHT TWIST Knit 2nd stitch on left needle in front of first stitch, then knit first stitch; slip both stitches off needle.

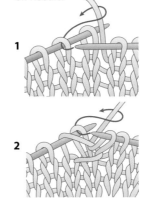

1

2

3

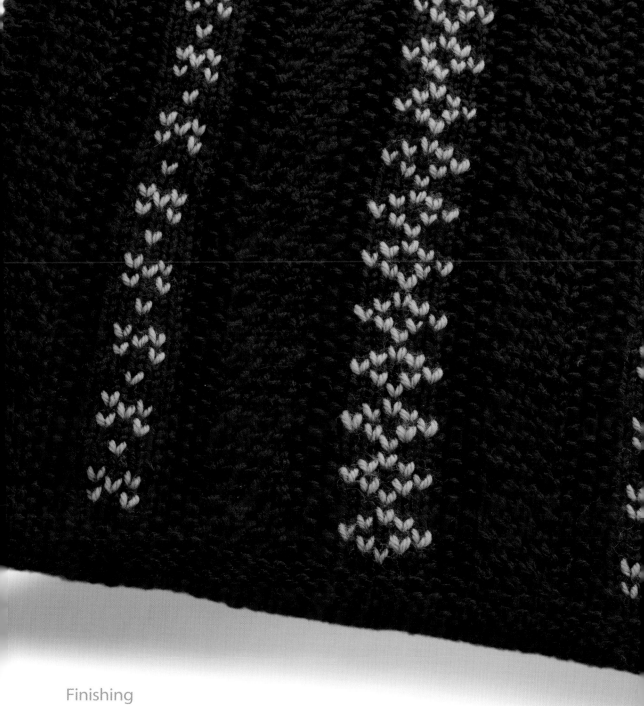

Finishing

Work duplicate stitch, over 5-stitch stockinette stitch columns following Charts A and B.

DUPLICATE STITCH

Little accents of color can be added after a piece is knit. This process is called duplicate stitch (also known as Swiss darning) and is worked as follows: with a blunt tapestry needle threaded with a length of yarn of a contrasting color, cover a knitted stitch with an embroidered stitch of the same shape. Photo below shows wrong side of square.

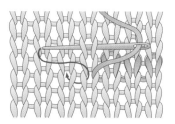

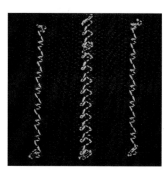

Svetlana Avrakh

TORONTO, ONTARIO, CANADA

Originally I came from Latvia. People say that all Latvian girls are born with needles in their hands, because we all know how to knit. I have knit and crocheted for as long as I can remember.

In this afghan square I combined my love for my daughter Anna, knitting, and colors. I cast on for the center square using invisible cast-on. This avoids extra bulk when picking up stitches for the Trinity stitch panels. Trinity Stitch is one of my favorite stitches for afghans because it is textural and dynamic in appearance. Corner cables were the perfect solution to joining the textured panels.

INTERMEDIATE+

featuring
invisible cast-on
pick up and knit
cables
duplicate stitch

MC Indigo
A Ruby Red
B Purple
C Gold
D Avocado

5mm /US 8
or size to obtain gauge

cable needle (cn)
stitch holders

Note *See page 28 for unfamiliar abbreviations and techniques.*

INC 1 Increase by knitting into front and back of stitch.

Center square

With MC, cast on 27 using invisible cast-on. *Row 1* (RS) K1, yo, k2tog, knit to last 3 stitches, SSK, yo, k1. *2* P2tog, yo, purl to last 2 stitches, yo, SSP. Work last 2 rows 15 more times. Cut MC.

PANEL 1

Row 1 (RS) Slip 2 stitches and place them on hold, then with A, k23, slip 2 stitches and place them on hold. *2* (WS) Inc 1 in first stitch, **[k2, Inc 1]** 7 times, Inc 1 in last stitch (9 stitches increased)—32 stitches. *3* Inc 1, p1, **[p1-k1-p1 in next stitch, p3tog]** to last 2 stitches, p1, Inc 1—34 stitches. *4* Inc 1, knit to last stitch, Inc 1—36 stitches. *5* Inc 1, p3, **[p3tog, (p1, k1, p1) in next stitch]** to last 4 stitches, p3, Inc 1—38 stitches. *6* Repeat Row 4—40 stitches. *7–14* Repeat Rows 3–6 twice. *15 and 16* Repeat Rows 3 and 4—60 stitches. Place all stitches on hold. Cut yarn.

PANEL 2

Remove waste yarn from cast-on edge of center square and place stitches on needle ready to work a RS row. With B, work as for Panel 1.

PANEL 3

With RS facing and C, pick up and knit 23 stitches along left side of center square, beginning and ending 2 rows in from edges. Work as for Panel 1, beginning with Row 2.

PANEL 4

With D, work as for Panel 3 along right side of center square.

CORNER 1

Begin all corner panels with RS facing and MC.
K2 from top left corner holder, then pick up and knit 2 along upper left side of

square—4 stitches. *Row 1* (WS) **[Inc 1]** 4 times—8 stitches. *2* Cast on 1, knit to end. *3* Cast on 1, purl to end—10 stitches. Work Rows 1–4 of Chart A 5 times, then work Rows 5–8. Fasten off.

Work corners 2, 3, and 4 to correspond, picking up 2 stitches along side of center square and knitting 2 from holders, following diagram.

BORDER

With RS facing and B, pick up and knit 5 along top of Corner 2, place 60 stitches from Panel 1 on needle, k3, **[k2tog, k2]** across, end k1, pick up and knit 5 along top of Corner 1—56 stitches. Turn. Bind off.

Work other edges to correspond, using D for left edge, A for lower edge, and C for right edge.

Work duplicate stitch in design of your choice as in Chart B.

IN OTHER WORDS

2/2 RC Slip 2 to cable needle, hold to back, k2; k2 from cable needle.

2/2 LC Slip 2 to cable needle, hold to front, k2; k2 from cable needle.

Chart A

Row 1 (RS) K1, p1, 2/2 RC, k2, p1, k1. *2 and 4* P1, k1, p6, k1, p1. *3* K1, p1, k2, 2/2 LC, p1, k1. Work Rows 1–4 four more times. *5* SSK, 2/2 RC, k2, k2tog. *6* P2tog, p4, SSP. *7* SSK, k2, k2tog. *8* P2tog, SSP.

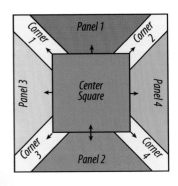

Chart A

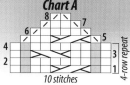

8
7
6
5
4
3
2
1

10 stitches

4-row repeat

Stitch key

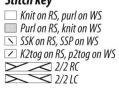

☐ Knit on RS, purl on WS
☐ Purl on RS, knit on WS
◩ SSK on RS, SSP on WS
◪ K2tog on RS, p2tog on WS
⬚ 2/2 RC
⬚ 2/2 LC

Color key

■ Indigo
■ Ruby Red
■ Purple
■ Gold
■ Avocado

Chart B

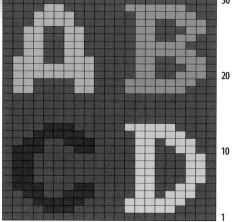

30

20

10

1

21 stitches

2/2 RIGHT CROSS (2/2 RC)

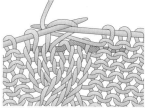

2/2 LEFT CROSS (2/2 LC)

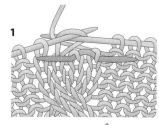

1

2

PICK UP AND KNIT HORIZONTALLY

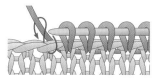

Along a horizontal edge, insert needle into center of every stitch.

PICK UP AND KNIT VERTICALLY

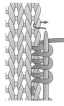

Along a vertical edge, insert needle into center of stitch, catch yarn and knit a stitch. *Example shows picking up 3 stitches for every 4 rows of stockinette stitch.*

Ginger Luters

GRASS VALLEY, CALIFORNIA

Although I'm not a quilter, I'm continually fascinated by patchwork quilt patterns. This whirligig pattern seems especially appropriate for a child's afghan. It reminds me of the pinwheels I loved as a child. This square is constructed in the same way a quilter would make a quilt block. However, instead of cutting and sewing triangles of fabric, you knit each triangle, joining it to previous triangles by picking up stitches. This block can be repeated for an afghan of any size. If you change the placement of the colors, you'll achieve a different effect. Another variation is to mirror-image the blocks to create an entirely new design.

Note *See page 28 for unfamiliar abbreviations and techniques. See page 9 for pick up and knit.*

See page 28 for unfamiliar abbreviations and techniques. See page 9 for pick up and knit.

GARTER RIDGE PATTERN

Row 1 (WS) Knit. *2 and 4* Knit. *3* Purl. Repeat Rows 1–4.

Square

TRIANGLE 1

With A, cast on 35. *Begin garter ridge pattern and decreases: Row 1* (WS) Knit. *2 and 4* K1, SSK, knit to last 3 stitches, k2tog, k1. *3* Purl. Work Rows 1–4 six more times, then work Rows 1–3 once—5 stitches. *Next row* (RS) K1, S2KP2, k1. *Next row* P3. *Next row* S2KP2. Fasten off.

TRIANGLE 2

With RS facing and B, pick up and knit 25 along right side of Triangle 1, from base to top. **[Work Rows 1–4 of Triangle 1]** 5 times, then work Row 1 once—5 stitches. Complete as for Triangle 1.

TRIANGLE 3

With RS facing and C, pick up and knit 18 along left side of Triangle 2, from top to base. *Begin garter ridge pattern and decreases: Row 1* (WS) Knit. *2 and 4* Knit to last 3 stitches, k2tog, k1. *3* Purl. Repeat Rows 1–4 six more times, then work Rows 1–3 once—3 stitches. *Next row* (RS) K2tog, k1. *Next row* P2tog. Fasten off.

TRIANGLE 4

With RS facing and A, pick up and knit 35 along sides of Triangles 2 and 3. Work as for Triangle 1.

TRIANGLES 5 AND 6

Work to correspond to Triangles 2 and 3.

TRIANGLES 7, 8, 9; AND 10, 11, 12

Work to correspond to Triangles 4, 5, and 6. Sew side edges of Triangles 11 and 12 to cast-on edge of Triangle 1, working from outside edge to center. At center, run yarn through center points of all triangles and pull up slightly.

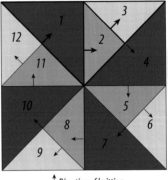

↑ *Direction of knitting*

Triangles

Building with triangles is easy, just take it one step at a time.

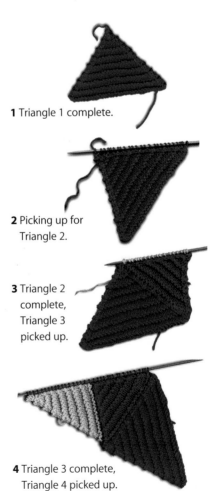

1 Triangle 1 complete.

2 Picking up for Triangle 2.

3 Triangle 2 complete, Triangle 3 picked up.

4 Triangle 3 complete, Triangle 4 picked up.

SSK

A left-slanting single decrease.

1 Slip 2 stitches separately to right needle as if to knit.

2 Knit these 2 stitches together by slipping left needle into them from left to right.

S2KP2, Sl2-K1-P2SSO

A centered double decrease.

1 Slip 2 stitches together to right needle as if to knit.

2 Knit next stitch.

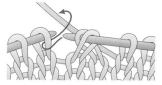

3 Pass 2 slipped stitches over knit stitch and off right needle.

4 Completed: 3 stitches become 1; the center stitch is on top.

Border

With RS facing, circular needle and B, begin where Triangles 1 and 2 meet and pick up and knit as follows: 25 stitches along Triangle 1, place marker (pm), 1 stitch in corner, **[50 stitches to next corner, pm, 1 stitch in corner]** 3 times, 25 stitches to starting point, pm for beginning of round — 204 stitches. *Round 1* **[Purl to marker, slip marker, k1]** 4 times, purl to end. *2* **[Knit to marker, yo, slip marker, k1, yo]** 4 times, knit to end. Work Rounds 1 and 2 once more. Bind off purlwise.

Kristin Nicholas

LEYDEN, MAINE

As a mother, I was constantly looking for ways to entertain and teach my daughter Julia. Children love to learn new things and are fascinated by pockets and containers of any kind. For my afghan square, I chose to make a pocket square with a flap that is perfect for keeping a child's toys. I made some knit shapes in bright colors to teach a child about different shapes and colors. I can also envision a child using the pocket square for keeping his or her favorite little toys or stuffed animals. This idea could be expanded: six squares could be made in different colors and attached together in a cube shape. Many pockets and different openings could be added. Attach zippers, buttonholes, laces, and more closures to each pocket and a child could use this as a knitted toy to learn about all kinds of fastenings. An older sibling might even learn to knit and make one of the garter stitch squares.

Note *See page 28 for unfamiliar abbreviations and techniques.*

INC 1 Increase by knitting into front and back of stitch.

Square

With MC, cast on 54. Knit 6 rows (3 ridges garter stitch), end with a WS row. *Row 1* (RS) Knit. *2* K3, p48, k3. Repeat last 2 rows until piece measures 11¼". Knit 6 rows. Bind off.

Pocket

With A, cast on 36. Work in garter stitch (knit every row), until piece measures 7½". Bind off.

Pocket flap

With B, cast on 36. Knit 10 rows (5 ridges garter stitch). *Next row* **[K2tog, knit to last 2 stitches, k2tog]** 17 times—2 stitches. *Next row* K2tog. Cut yarn, leaving a 20" tail for button loop. With crochet hook, chain 2". Fasten off and form loop.

Shapes *make 2 of each*

SQUARE
With B, cast on 9. Knit 18 rows (9 ridges garter stitch). Bind off.

TRIANGLE
With C, cast on 13. Knit 2 rows. *Next 12 rows* K2tog, knit to end. Fasten off last stitch.

DIAMOND
With MC, cast on 2 stitches. *Next 11 rows* Inc 1, knit to end. *Next 2 rows* K13. *Next 11 rows* K2tog, knit to end. Bind off remaining 2 stitches.

CIRCLE
With C, cast on 6. Knit 2 rows. [*Next row* **Inc 1, knit to last stitch, Inc 1. Knit 1 row.**] 3 times. *Next 6 rows* K12. [*Next row* **K2tog, knit to last 2 stitches, k2tog. Knit 1 row.**] 3 times. *Next row* K6. Bind off.

Finishing

Sew shapes together, leaving an opening for stuffing. Stuff each shape with a small amount of yarn. Sew opening. Sew pocket to main square, placing it as shown in diagram. Sew pocket flap to main square. Sew on button.

EASY

featuring
shaping
seaming

MC Gold
A Purple
B Avocado
C Ruby Red

5mm/US 8
or size to obtain gauge

3 **5mm/US 8**

1 **1" (25mm)**

size H/8 (5mm)
crochet hook

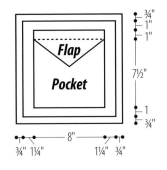

chain

1 Make slip knot, yarn over hook, draw yarn through loop on hook.

2 First chain made.

Sewing

Sewing on a pocket is easy if you just take it a stitch at a time. With a strand of yarn that matches the pocket, bring needle up through the background and through one stitch from the edge of the pocket, then sew downward into the background, one stitch over, and bring the yarn up 2 rows from before and repeat.

Joni Coniglio

LINCOLN, NEBRASKA

I became fascinated by knitting when I was about 10 years old and discovered knitting books public library.

I used entrelac (my favorite technique) in my square. But I wanted it to be as easy to work as possible. I've combined a simple 4-row houndstooth pattern with solid color squares. The pattern is so simple that you won't even need to follow instructions after awhile. And if you should want a bigger piece, you simply have to cast on a larger multiple of 12 stitches.

INTERMEDIATE

featuring
entrelac
pick up and knit

MC Ruby Red
CC Indigo

4mm/US 6

&

stitch holders

Notes 1 *See page 28 for unfamiliar abbreviations and techniques. See page 9 for pick up and knit.* 2 *Slip stitches purlwise with yarn at WS unless otherwise indicated.*

Square

With MC, cast on 46. Knit 6 rows (3 ridges garter stitch), decrease 4 stitches evenly across last (WS) row—42 stitches. *Next row* (RS) K3 and place these stitches on hold, knit to last 3 stitches and place them on hold.

Work over center 36 stitches as follows: *Work 3 base triangles: *Row 1* (WS) P2, turn. *2 and all RS rows* Knit to end of base triangle being worked. *3* P3, turn. *5* P4, turn. *7* P5, turn. *9–21* Continue to work 1 more purl stitch every WS row until there are 12 purl stitches on right needle, do not turn work after Row 21 (1 base triangle complete). Repeat from* twice more—3 base triangles. Turn work.

Work right-side triangle: Row 1 (RS) K2, turn. *2 and all WS rows* Purl. *3* K1, M1, SSK (1 stitch of side triangle together with 1 stitch of base triangle or MC rectangle), turn. *5* K1, M1, k1, SSK, turn. *7* K1, M1, k2, SSK, turn. *9* K1, M1, k3, SSK, turn. *11–21* Continue to work 1 more knit stitch between M1 and SSK every RS row until all stitches of base triangle (or MC rectangle) have been worked, do not turn work after Row 21.

Work 2 houndstooth rectangles *With RS facing and MC, pick up and k12 stitches along remaining side of base triangle (or MC rectangle). *Beg Houndstooth pattern: Rows 1 and 3* (WS) P12 with working color. *2* With CC, k1, **[slip 1, k2]** 3 times, slip 1, SSK (1 stitch of houndstooth rectangle together with 1 stitch of base

triangle or MC rectangle). *4* With MC, **[slip 1, k2]** 3 times, slip 1, k1, SSK. Work Rows 1–4 four more times, then work Rows 1–3 once. *Next row* (RS) With MC, k11, SSK. Repeat from * once more— 2 houndstooth rectangles. Cut CC.

Work left-side triangle With RS facing and MC, pick up and knit 12 stitches along remaining side of last base triangle (or MC rectangle). *Row 1* (WS) P2tog, p10. *2 and all RS rows* Knit. *3* P2tog, p9. *5* P2tog, p8. *7–19* Continue to work 1 less purl stitch after p2tog every WS row until 2 stitches remain. *21* P2tog, do not turn work.

Work 3 MC rectangles With WS facing and MC, pick up and purl 11 stitches along left-side triangle—12 stitches. ***Row 1* (RS) K12. *2* P11, p2tog (1 stitch from MC rectangle together with houndstooth rectangle) 12 times.* With WS facing, pick up and purl 12 stitches along houndstooth rectangle (or side triangle); repeat from ** once more, then work from ** to * once—3 MC rectangles. Continue working entrelac pattern as follows: *Work right-side triangle, 2 houndstooth pattern rectangles, then left-side triangle.* Work 3 MC rectangles. Work from * to * once more.

Work 3 top triangles *With WS facing and MC, pick up and purl 11 stitches along left-side triangle (or houndstooth rectangle)—12 stitches. *Row 1 and all RS rows* Knit. *2* P2tog, p9, p2tog (1 stitch of top triangle together with 1 stitch of houndstooth rectangle or right-side triangle). *4* P2tog, p8, p2tog. *6* P2tog, p7, p2tog. *8–18* Continue to work 1 less purl stitch between p2tog's every WS row until 3 triangle stitches remain. *Row 20* **[P2tog]** twice. *22* P3tog. *24* P2tog. Repeat from * twice more— 3 top triangles. Fasten off last stitch.

Finishing

SIDE BORDERS

With MC, pick up 3 stitches on hold at right side of square, ready to work a WS row. Knit. *Next row* (RS) K3, pick up and knit 1 from square, turn—4 stitches. *Next row* (WS) K2tog, k2—3 stitches. Repeat these 2 rows until edging has been worked up side edge of square. Put 3 edge stitches on hold. Repeat for left side EXCEPT pick up on the wrong-side of square.

TOP BORDERS

With RS facing, k3 stitches from right-side band on hold, pick up and k40 stitches evenly along top edge of square, k3 stitches from left-side band on hold—46 stitches. Knit 6 rows. Bind off.

 ↑ Direction of knitting

 Base triangle

 Right-side triangle

 Houndstooth rectangle

 Left-side triangle

 MC rectangle

Top triangle

PICK UP AND PURL

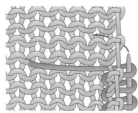

With wrong side facing and yarn in front, insert needle from back to front between first and second stitches, catch yarn, and purl.

Entrelac is worked in triangles and rectangles. The shapes are worked one at a time and attached to their neighbors as you knit.

Tier 1 Start work here with WS facing.

a Start a Base Triangle (BT) worked on 2 stitches and growing to 12 stitches.

b Continue until 3 BTs are worked across. All stitches are on needle.

Tier 2

Start work here with RS facing and a RS row.

a Make a right-side triangle (T1) starting with 2 stitches and growing to 12. At end of every RS row, work last stitch together with first stitch from BT3.

Start work here with a RS row.

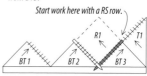

b For houndstooth rectangle (R1), pick up 12 stitches along edge of BT3. At end of every RS row, work last stitch together with first stitch from BT2.

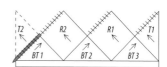

c Work a second rectangle (R2), then end with a left-side triangle (T2).

Tier 3

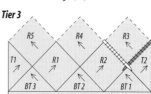

With WS facing, work 3 MC rectangles (R3, 4, 5).

15

Susan Mills

WEST TOWNSEND, MAINE

My mother taught me to knit as a child. (I remember knitting Barbie clothes that were triangular shaped because I split stitches and increased so often.) By the time I was in high school, I had forgotten how. Being at an age when I didn't listen to my mother, I taught myself from a book. As a result, I knit in a peculiar way—I hold the yarn in my left hand continental style, but wrap the yarn backwards on both knit and purl stitches. I've tried to re-teach myself to knit the correct way, but always revert back to my own old comfortable style mid-project.

My afghan square was inspired by the paper dolls that my daughter, Mackenzie made.

INTERMEDIATE

featuring
stranded 2-color knitting

MC Indigo
A Purple
B Ruby Red

5mm/US 8
or size to obtain gauge

Notes **1** *See page 28 for unfamiliar abbreviations and techniques.* **2** *Each 2-color row of the paperdoll chart is worked in a method called stranded 2-color knitting, where the yarn not in use is carried loosely across the wrong side.*

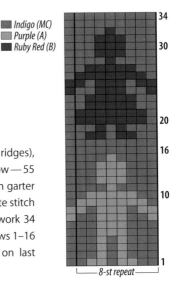

Indigo (MC)
Purple (A)
Ruby Red (B)

8-st repeat

Square

With MC, cast on 52. Knit 6 rows (3 garter ridges), increase 3 stitches evenly on last (WS) row — 55 stitches. Keeping first and last 3 stitches in garter stitch, work center 49 stitches in stockinette stitch (knit RS rows, purl WS rows) as follows: work 34 rows in Chart pattern, then work Chart Rows 1–16 once more, decrease 3 stitches evenly on last row — 52 stitches. Knit 6 rows. Bind off.

WEAVING THE CARRIES

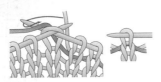

From the knit side
To weave the carry above a knit stitch: Insert needle into stitch and under woven yarn, then knit the stitch as usual.

From the purl side
To weave the carry above a purl stitch: Insert needle into stitch and under woven yarn, then purl the stitch as usual.

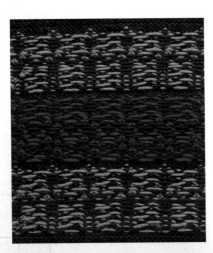

STRANDED 2-COLOR KNITTING

Two colors worked across a row form a color pattern: the unused color is carried (stranded) along the wrong side of the fabric. These 'carries' should not exceed 1 inch. Weave any carry longer than 1 inch along the wrong side. Carries should not be too tight or too loose so as not to affect the gauge or distort the fabric.

E. J. Slayton

CADET, MONTANA

My grandmother taught me to knit (probably in self-defense!) when I was about 9. My parents were stationed in Central America and I lived with my grandparents for a couple of years. My serious involvement with knitting came years later when I encountered Elizabeth Zimmermann's "Busy Knitter" series on PBS and her book Knitting Without Tears.

I particularly enjoy putting cables and texture patterns together, so I've combined the Heart Strings and Hugs & Kisses cables and bordered them with little knit and purl hearts for a square that's full of love.

Note *See page 28 for unfamiliar abbreviations and techniques.*

INC 1
Increase by purling into front and back of stitch.

Square
Cast on 56. Knit 6 rows (3 ridges garter stitch). *Foundation row 1* (RS) K7, M1, k4, p2, **[k2, M1]** twice, k2, **[p2, inc 1)]** twice, p2, **[k1, M1]** twice, **[p2, Inc 1]** twice, p2, **[k2, M1]** twice, k2, p2, k4, M1, k7 — 68 stitches. *2* K3, p9, k2, p8, k10, p4, k10, p8, k2, p9, k3.
Begin chart patterns: Row 1 (RS) K3, work Chart A, p2, Chart B, place marker (pm), Chart C, pm, Chart B, p2, Chart A, k3. *2* K3, work Chart A, k2, Chart B, Chart C, Chart B, k2, Chart A, k3. Continue as established until 32 rows of Chart C have been worked twice, then work Rows 1–6 once — 68 stitches.
Decrease row (RS) K5, k2tog, k5, p2, k1, SSK, k2, k2tog, k1, p1, SSP, p3, p2tog, p2, SSK, k2tog, p2, SSP, p3, p2tog, p1, k1, SSK, k2, k2tog, k1, p2, k5, k2tog, k5 — 56 stitches. Knit 6 rows, binding off on last WS row.

INTERMEDIATE

featuring
cable patterns

Deep Denim

10cm/4"

30 **32**

over Chart C

4mm/US 6
or size to obtain gauge

&

cable needle (cn)
stitch markers

Chart A
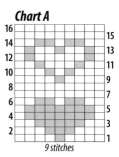
9 stitches

Chart B
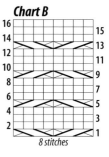
8 stitches

Pattern Arrangement

K3 sts	9 sts Chart A	P2 sts	8 sts Chart B	24 sts Chart C	8 sts Chart B	P2 sts	9 sts Chart A	K3 sts
				68 stitches				

Chart C

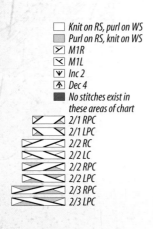

Knit on RS, purl on WS
Purl on RS, knit on WS
M1R
M1L
Inc 2
Dec 4
No stitches exist in
these areas of chart
2/1 RPC
2/1 LPC
2/2 RC
2/2 LC
2/2 RPC
2/2 LPC
2/3 RPC
2/3 LPC

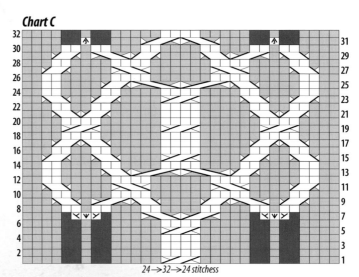

24→32→24 stitchess

IN OTHER WORDS

INC 2 Knit into back and front of stitch, then insert left needle behind vertical strand between the 2 stitches just made, knit this strand through back loop (see illustration).

DEC 4 Slip 3 with yarn in front, * pass 2nd stitch on right needle over first (center) stitch, slip center stitch back to left needle and pass 2nd stitch on left needle over it,* slip center stitch to right needle, repeat from * to * once more, purl center stitch.

2/1 RPC Slip 1 to cn, hold to back, k2; p1 from cn.
2/1 LPC Slip 2 to cn, hold to front, p1; k2 from cn.
2/2 RC Slip 2 to cn, hold to back, k2; k2 from cn.
2/2 LC Slip 2 to cn, hold to front, k2; k2 from cn.
2/2 RPC Slip 2 to cn, hold to back, k2; p2 from cn.
2/2 LPC Slip 2 to cn, hold to front, p2; k2 from cn.
2/3 RPC Slip 3 to cn, hold to back, k2; p3 from cn.
2/3 LPC Slip 2 to cn, hold to front, p3; k2 from cn.

Chart A *over 9 stitches*

Row 1 (RS) K4, p1, k4. *2* P3, k3, p3. *3* K2, p5, k2. *4* P1, k7, p1. *5* K1, p7, k1. *6* P2, k2, p1, k2, p2. *7* Knit. *8* Purl. *9* Repeat Row 1. *10* P3, k1, p1, k1, p3. *11* K2, p1, k3, p1, k2. *12* P1, k1, p5, k1, p1. *13* K1, p1, **[k2, p1]** twice, k1. *14–16* Repeat Rows 6–8. Repeat Rows 1–16.

Chart B *over 8 stitches*

Row 1 (RS) 2/2 RC, 2/2 LC. *2 and all WS rows* P8. *3, 7, 11, and 15* K8. *5 and 9* 2/2 LC, 2/2 RC. *13* Repeat Row 1. *16* Repeat Row 2. Repeat Rows 1–16.

Chart C *24 stitches, increased to 32 stitches, decreased back to 24 stitches*

Rows 1 and 5 (RS) P10, 2/2 RC, p10. *2 and all WS rows (except 8)* Knit the knit stitches and purl the purl stitches. *3* P10, k4, p10. *7* P4, *M1R, Inc 2, M1L,* p3, 2/2 RPC, 2/2 LPC, p3, work from *to* once, p4—32 stitches. *8* K4, p2, k1, p2, k3, p2, k4, p2, k3, p2, k1, p2, k4. *9* P3, 2/1 RPC, p1, 2/2 LPC, 2/1 RPC, p4, 2/1 LPC, 2/2 RPC, p1, 2/1 LPC, p3. *11* P2, 2/1 RPC, p4, 2/2 LC, p6, 2/2 LC, p4, 2/1 LPC, p2. *13* P2, k2, p4, 2/1 RPC, 2/3 LPC, 2/3 RPC, 2/1 LPC, p4, k2, p2. *15* P2, 2/1 LPC, p2, 2/1 RPC, p4, 2/2 RC, p4, 2/1 LPC, p2, 2/1 RPC, p2. *17* P3, 2/1 LPC, 2/1 RPC, p5, k4, p5, 2/1 LPC, 2/1 RPC, p3. *19* P4, 2/2 RC, **[p6, 2/2 RC]** twice, p4. *21* P3, 2/1 RPC, 2/1 LPC, p5, k4, p5, 2/1 RPC, 2/1 LPC, p3. *23* P2, 2/1 RPC, p2, 2/1 LPC, p4, 2/2 RC, p4, 2/1 RPC, p2, 2/1 LPC, p2. *25* P2, k2, p4, 2/1 LPC, 2/3 RPC, 2/3 LPC, 2/1 RPC, p4, k2, p2. *27* P2, 2/1 LPC, p4, 2/2 LC, p6, 2/2 LC, p4, 2/1 RPC, p2. *29* P3, 2/1 LPC, p1, 2/2 RPC, 2/1 LPC, p4, 2/1 RPC, 2/2 LPC, p1, 2/1 RPC, p3. *31* P4, Dec 4, p3, 2/2 LPC, 2/2 RPC, p3, Dec 4, p4—24 stitches. *32* Repeat Row 2. Repeat Rows 1–32.

9

Janet Szabo

KALISPELL, MONTANA

Although my mother taught me how to knit when I was about 8, I didn't knit seriously until my college days. There I knit all the time. I only had one knitting book and everything I made came out of it. Some of my friends are still wearing those sweaters 15 years later!

I almost always approach designing from a technical angle, and it's taken a while to loosen up my creative side. I am convinced, though, that technical mastery is a key element of good design.

I have two terrific daughters: Mariah and Ellen. Both girls share my passion for gardening, and that is how I came up with the idea for this square. It seemed natural to combine intarsia cables and embroidered vines, flowers, and leaves. I love the bright, primary colors, and I wanted to use all of them in my design, so I created a "fantasy" plant with flowers of three different colors (see Embroidery Diagram). **EDITOR'S NOTE** *Our fantasy went to butterflies and dragonflies.*

INTERMEDIATE +

featuring
intasia cables
embroidery

MC Gold
A Indigo
B Avocado
C Ruby Red
D Purple
E Deep Denim

5mm/US 8
or size to obtain gauge

3.75mm/ F-5

&

cable needle (cn)
sharp tapestry needle
bobbins

Notes

1 *See page 28 for unfamiliar abbreviations and techniques. See page 4 for intarsia and page 9 for cable basics.* **2** *Use 7 bobbins of A, one for each rib of trellis.* **3** *The background color will strand behind the trellises.*

Square

With MC, cast on 56. Knit 6 rows (3 ridges garter stitch). *Next row* (RS) K13, k30 and increase 5 stitches evenly across, k13 — 61 stitches. *Begin Chart: Row 1* (WS) K13, work Chart over 35 stitches, k13. *2* K3, p10, work Chart, p10, k3. Continue to work center 35 stitches in Chart, 10 stitches each side of Chart in reverse Stockinette stitch, and 3 stitches at each edge in garter stitch, through Chart Row 16, then work Rows 1–16 three more times. Work Rows 1–8. Cut A. *Next row* (WS) With MC, knit the knit stitches and purl the purl stitches, and decrease 5 stitches across center 35 stitches — 56 stitches. Knit 6 rows. Bind off.

IN OTHER WORDS

2/1 RPC Slip 1 to cable needle, hold to back, k2A; p1MC from cable needle.
2/1 LPC Slip 2 to cable needle, hold to front, p1MC; k2A from cable needle.
2/2 RC With A, slip 2 to cable needle, hold to back, k2; k2 from cable needle.
2/2 LC With A, slip 2 to cable needle, hold to front, k2; k2 from cable needle.

Chart *over 35 stitches*

Row 1 (WS) K1MC, **[p2A, k4MC, p2A, k2MC]** 3 times, p2A, k2MC. *2* P1MC, **[2/1 RPC, p2MC, 2/1 LPC, p2MC]** 3 times, 2/1 RPC, p1MC. *3* K2MC, **[p2A, k2MC, p2A, k4MC]** 3 times, p2A, k1MC. *4* **[2/1 RPC, p4MC, 2/1 LPC]** 3 times, 2/1 RPC, p2MC. *5 and 7* K3MC, **[p4A, k6MC]** 3 times, p2A. *6* K2A, **[p6MC, 2/2 RC]** 3 times, p3MC. *8* **[2/1 LPC, p4MC, 2/1 RPC]** 3 times, 2/1 LPC, p2MC. *9* K2MC, **[p2A, k2MC, p2A, k4MC]** 3 times, p2A, k1MC. *10* P1MC, **[2/1 LPC, p2MC, 2/1 RPC, p2MC]** 3 times, 2/1 LPC, p1MC. *11* K1MC, **[p2A, k4MC, p2A, k2MC]** 3 times, p2A, k2MC. *12* P2MC, **[2/1 LPC, 2/1 RPC, p4MC]** 3 times, 2/1 LPC. *13 and 15* P2A, **[k6MC, p4A]** 3 times, k3MC. *14* P3MC, **[2/2 LC, p6MC]** 3 times, k2A. *16* P2MC, **[2/1 RPC, 2/1 LPC, p4MC]** 3 times, 2/1 RPC. Repeat Rows 1–16 for Chart.

☐ With A, knit on RS, purl on WS
▨ With MC, purl on RS, knit on WS
▱ 2/1 RPC
▱ 2/1 LPC
▱ 2/2 RC
▱ 2/2 LC

Chart

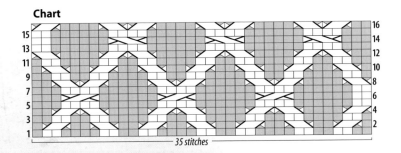

35 stitches

Butterflies and dragonflies

Work bullion-stitch bodies, French-knot heads, and lazy-daisy wings.

 Bullion with B or C

 Lazy Daisy with D or E (work French Knot for head with 2 plies)

Embroidery Diagram

 Crochet Chain with B

Chain continued under trellis

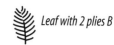 Leaf with 2 plies B

 Stems with 2 plies B

 Lazy Daisy with C, D or E (work French Knot in center with 2 plies A)

Lazy Daisy

Stem Stitch

French Knot

Leaf Stitch

Bullion Stitch

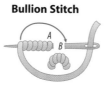

21

Edie Eckman

WAYNESBORO, VIRGINIA

My grandmother lived with us when I was growing up, and she and my mother were always working on some sort of needlework or sewing project. When my children Meg and Charlie were born, I wanted to find a way for them to have the same exposure to needlework. Two old-fashioned toys — a wooden sewing board with holes and colored shoelaces, and a mushroom-shaped knitting knobby used to make knit cord — served that purpose.

This afghan square was inspired by those toys. The background is a fairly simple pattern stitch and works up quickly. The colored I-cords can be made in colors of your choice and in assorted lengths. The designs can be arranged as desired. These cords can be made on double-pointed needles. Better yet, get out a knitting knobby or cord-making machine and let the kids help!

Note *See page 28 for unfamiliar abbreviations and techniques.*

Square

With MC, cast on 55. Knit 6 rows (3 ridges garter stitch), end with a WS row. Keeping 3 stitches each side in garter stitch (knit every row), work center 49 stitches in Chart pattern until 12 rows of chart have been worked 6 times, then work Rows 1–5 once more. Knit 6 rows. Bind off.

I-CORD TIES *Make 4 in CC of your choice*

With dpn, cast on 3. Work 20" I-cord. Bind off. Thread tie through holes of square. Knot ends.

IN OTHER WORDS

Chart pattern *multiple of 8 stitches, plus 1*

Rows 1 and 5 (RS) K1, **[p3, k5]** across. *2 and 4* **[P5, k3]** to last stitch, p1. *3* K1, **[p1, yo, p2tog, k5]** across. *6* Purl. *7 and 11* **[K5, p3]** to last stitch, k1. *8 and 10* P1, **[k3, p5]** across. *9* **[K5, p1, yo, p2tog]** to last stitch, k1. *12* Purl. Repeat Rows 1–12 for Chart pattern.

EASY

featuring
I-cord

MC Gold
CC 1 Ruby Red
CC 2 Deep Denim
CC 3 Avocado

5mm/US 8
or size to obtain gauge

2 **5mm/US 8**

Yo before a purl stitch

With yarn in front of needle, bring yarn over needle and to front again, purl next stitch.

p2tog

With yarn in front of needle, purl 2 stitches at the same time.

I-cord

I-cord is a tiny tube of stockinette stitch, made with 2 double-pointed needles.
1 Cast on 3 or 4 stitches.
2 Knit. Do not turn work. Slide stitches to opposite end of needle. Repeat Step 2 until cord is the desired length.

Chart

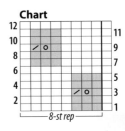

☐ Knit on RS, purl on WS
▨ Purl on RS, knit on WS
⊡ Yo
⊘ P2tog

Lucy Neatby

DARTMOUTH, NOVA SCOTIA, CANADA

The mechanics of knitting I learned from my mother and grandmother as a child, but true passion began when I discovered color and texture in yarns. Armed with my knitting and a sextant, I set off to sea for a six-month trip! I found myself aground and as a means to hang on to my sanity when the children were small, I knit constantly on more and more challenging pieces.

All children love surprises. Lurking under each button-up flap is a little treasure. I've chosen something to represent the interest of each of my children, but the embroidered letters of a name or pretty buttons, bells, or mirrors could also be used and with the addition of extra flaps, a memory puzzle, color, or alphabet recognition game could be created.

Notes 1 *See page 28 for unfamiliar abbreviations and techniques. See page 4 for intarsia basics.* **2** *Use separate lengths of yarn for blocks of color.*

Square

With A, cast on 54. Knit 6 rows (3 ridges garter stitch), end with a WS row. Keeping 3 stitches at each side in garter stitch (knit every row) with A, work center 48 stitches in stockinette stitch (knit on RS, purl on WS) as follows: Work 7 rows with MC. *Next row* (WS) 34MC, p8B, p6MC. Work 10 rows more, maintaining colors. Work 8 rows with MC. *Next row* (RS) K20MC, k8A, k20MC. Work 10 rows more, maintaining colors. Work 8 rows with MC. *Next row* (WS) P6MC, p8C, p34MC. Work 10 rows more, maintaining colors. Work 7 rows with MC. With A, knit 6 rows. Bind off.

Finishing

Block piece.

Flaps

With dpn and D, cast on 10 stitches. Knit 2 rows. *Next row* (RS) K3, SSK, yo, k2tog, k3. *Next row* K4, knit into front and back of yo (buttonhole complete), k4. Knit 14 rows. *Next row* (RS) K9, knit last stitch with 1 strand each of B and D held together. Cut

D. Work attached I-cord as follows: With free dpn, slip B part of last stitch worked, slide stitch to opposite end of dpn, loop cast on 1 stitch, then pick up and knit 1 stitch in first ridge along edge of flap, *slide stitches to opposite end of dpn, with 3rd dpn, k1, k2tog tbl, pick up and knit 1 stitch from edge (see illustration); repeat from * around, working 2 rows of unattached I-cord at corners (k2, slide stitches to opposite end of dpn). When edging is complete, pass 2nd B stitch over first stitch, then slip first D stitch from left dpn to right dpn, pass remaining B stitch over this stitch. Slip D stitch back to left dpn. Attach flap over B square as follows: With D, make a slip knot on crochet hook. Insert hook from back of square through stitch 1 row above and 1 stitch to right of B square. Pull first D stitch from dpn through. Yo hook and pull through both loops on hook. Continue in this manner, working across top of B square, until all D stitches have been worked, ending 1 stitch to left of B square. Make 2 more flaps, using A and C for edging. Attach flaps to matching color squares. Sew 1 button on each square, under buttonhole. Attach hidden treasure on each square.

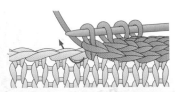

Attached I-cord
Slide stitches to opposite end of dpn and k1, then k2tog through the back loops, pick up and knit 1 stitch from edge. Repeat Row 2 for I-cord.

EASY +

featuring
**simple intarsia
attached I-cord**

MC Purple
A Ruby Red
B Gold
C Avocado
D Deep Denim

5mm/US 8
or size to obtain gauge

3 **5mm/US 8**

Optional **3 treasure buttons**

&

size H/8 (5mm)
crochet hook

12

Mary Lou Eastman

LINCOLN, NEBRASKA

Knitting-related activities take a major amount of my time. While it has not always been that way, I have nearly always had a knitting project in progress. My mother taught me to knit when I was four and I remember knitting up that same multicolored ball of leftovers many times (my mom still has it). In my square, I tried to incorporate color, texture, shape, and simplicity.

Note *See page 28 for unfamiliar abbreviations and techniques. See page 4 for intarsia basics.*

Square

With MC, cast on 54. Knit 6 rows (3 ridges garter stitch). Keeping first and last 3 stitches in garter stitch (knit every row) with MC, work center 48 stitches as follows: Work Pattern stitch, AT SAME TIME, work intarsia, following diagram for stitches and rows of each color. When 62 rows of Pattern stitch have been worked, knit 6 rows with MC. Bind off.

EASY +

featuring
simple intarsia

MC Purple
A Ruby Red
B Avocado
C Deep Denim
D Gold
E Indigo

5mm/US 8
or size to obtain gauge

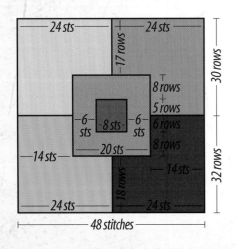

IN OTHER WORDS

WRAP STITCH Yo, p2, pass yo over p2.
PATTERN STITCH *multiple of 4 stitches*
Rows 1, 3, 5 and 7 (RS) Knit.
2 and 6 Purl.
4 **[Wrap stitch, p2]** across. *8* **[P2, Wrap stitch]** across. Repeat Rows 1–8 for Pattern stitch.

Pattern Stitch

4-stitch repeat

☐ Knit on RS, purl on WS
⌣ Wrap stitch

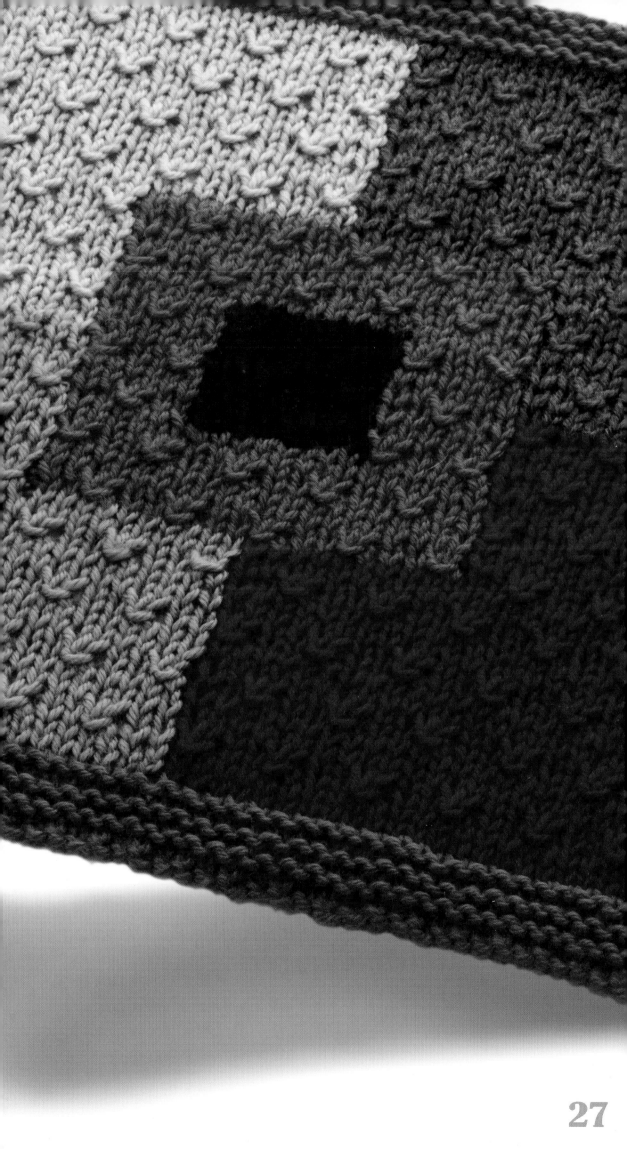

abbreviations

b in back of stitch
CC contrasting color
cn cable needle
cm centimeter(s)
dec decreas(e)(ed)(es)(ing)
dpn double pointed needle(s)
g gram(s)
" inch(es)
inc increas(e)(ed)(es)(ing)
k knit(ting)(s)(ted)
M1 make one
m meter(s)
MC main color
oz ounce(s)
p purl(ed)(ing)(s)
pm place marker
PSSO pass slipped stitch(es) over
RS right side(s)
sc single crochet
sl slip(ped)(ping)
SKP slip, knit, psso
SSK slip, slip, knit 2tog
st(s) stitch(es)
St st stockinette stitch
tbl through back of loop(s)
tog together
WS wrong side(s)
wyib with yarn in back
wyif with yarn in front
yd yard(s)
yo (2) yarn over (twice)

---

metrics

To convert the inches measurements used in our instructions to centimeters, simply multiply the inches by 2.5.
For example: 4" x 2.5 = 10cm

Charts and symbols

Our charts show the right side (RS) of the fabric. In general, each "square" is a stitch; a row of squares represents a row (or round) of stitches. Heavy lines on the charts are used to define pattern repeats.

RS. When facing the RS of the fabric, read the chart from right to left as you work and work the stitches as the symbols indicate. If you are working circularly, work every round thus.

WS. If you are working back and forth in rows, every other row will be a wrong side (WS) row. Read WS rows from left to right as you work.

Knitter's School

Loop cast-on

Often used to cast on a few stitches for a buttonhole. Loops can be formed over the index finger or thumb and can slant to the left or to the right. On the next row, work through back loop of right-slanting loops.

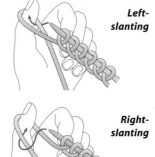

Left-slanting

Right-slanting

Make 1 (M1) Knit

Uses. A single increase. (If instructions don't specify, use M1 knit, either left- or right-slanting.)

For a left-slanting increase **M1L**, insert left needle from front to back under strand between last stitch knitted and first stitch on left needle. Knit, twisting strand by working into loop at back of needle.

The result is a left-slanting increase.

Or, for a right-slanting increase **M1R**, insert left needle from back to front under strand between last stitch knitted and first stitch on left needle. Knit, twisting strand by working into loop at front of needle.

The result is a right slanting increase.

Invisible cast-on

Uses. As a *temporary cast on*, when access to the bottom loops is needed.

1. Knot working yarn to contrasting waste yarn. With needle in right hand, hold knot in right hand. Tension both strands in left hand; separate the strands with fingers of the left hand. Yarn over with working yarn in front of waste strand.

2. Holding waste strand taut, pivot yarns and yarn over with working yarn in back of waste strand.
3. Each yarn over forms a stitch. Alternate yarn over in front and in back of waste strand for required number of stitches. For an even number, twist working yarn around waste strand before knitting the first row.
4. Later, untie knot, remove waste strand, and arrange bottom loops on needle.

Yarn over (yo)

Between knit stitches
Bring yarn under the needle to the front, take it over the needle to the back and knit the next stitch.

Completed yo increase.

Unattached I-cord

I-cord is a tiny tube of stockinette stitch, made with 2 double-pointed needles.
1. Cast on 3 (or more) stitches.
2. *Knit 3 (or more). Do not turn work. Slide stitches to right end of needle. Repeat from* for desired length. The tube forms as the yarn is pulled across the back of each row.